I0473403

Memorabilia Madness

How I created, marketed, a memorabilia and art print business

©Thomas Roth Jr.

Missing Toe Publishing 2013

Chester SC USA

No part of this book may be reproduced or transmitted in any form or by any means, electronic, mechanical, including photocopy, recording or any information storage retrieval system, without consent of the author.

Contents

Memorabilia Madness

Introduction

Welcome to the world of memorabilia products and marketing. This is a world where creativity and marketing collide. This is a business world that can be fun and challenging. The memorabilia business is all around you, and that's great news.

Do you travel, live near a national park, or some historical event, and then you are very familiar with the memorabilia business. Travel to any seaside location and you will see art prints, postcards, and much more, that's memorabilia, and most was not created and sold by a giant conglomerate.

When I realized that there is plenty of room for the creative entrepreneur, I knew I had to create and build a memorabilia business. This is my story.

Who you are

My guess is that you are some type of creative person. I guess that you enjoy the products of the memorabilia business, because you have purchased many of these products yourself. Many times you have stood in the gift shop and said to yourself, "I could this." I am sure many people have said this to themselves but, few have started or even attempted at creating a memorabilia business.

It is true that many skills are needed to create, market and sell memorabilia and art products but , do not let that stop you from creating your own business. Do not let the lack of cash stop you, many of the products I discuss are affordable to make. If you are still interested in learning about the memorabilia, art print business then maybe I can help.

Who am I

I am a photographer for over forty years. I was first published at age fifteen. Photography has always been an outlet for me. When I retired from the wholesale floral distribution business, thirteen years ago I entered full time into the photography business. I enjoy photography now more than ever due to the digital development of photography. Combine digital capture with the internet and new software there is new life in my photography.

I am a business person. I have owned several businesses over the last thirty years. I love buying and selling products. Thirty three years I was in the wholesale floral distribution business, and was able to transfer many of the skills I learned to my new business.

I am a traveler. I enjoy visiting all type of locations, and when I travel I collect memorabilia from the places I visit. It's not just me when I am out about that collect memorabilia; I have seen everyone picking up some sort of a reminder of where they have been. It is when I see people buying postcards, greeting cards, and prints, that my love of photography and business compel me to start a memorabilia and print business.

I live in a small rural southern town of six thousand people with a total of thirty thousand in the county. The area is rich in history and culture. One of the main routes from northern United States to the south is interstate seventy seven. The history, culture, state parks and massive traffic on the interstate lead me to believe that I could create a memorabilia business, and grow it into a profitable enterprise.

What you can learn from this book

I have written this book in hopes that you may create a solid foundation to launch your business: That you can take the lessons that I have learned and improve upon them to create a thriving Memorabilia business.

The many skills needed may be learned or you can hire people to do the work for you. Do remember that this is a **business!** Every dime you spend detracts from your profits.

From this book you will learn that the memorabilia business is a very large industry: but has plenty of room for the industrious creative person. You will learn that the memorabilia industry is a very exciting, and creative industry, but is also a business that is concerned with profits.

I have learned that there are many companies that produce products of the type I want to sell. However I found these companies are interested in tourist areas. My location is not a tourist attraction. I have considered, as someone reading this book may do, and that is to deal with these companies as an image or verse supplier.

Greeting card producers and distributors are always looking for fresh images and verse. Many of the companies that I researched had submission guidelines and forms, making it easy to submit my work. This book is not about how to get my images and verse with large distributors, but how to produce products in a small quantity at a profit.

This is the best time for disclaimer. These are my experiences with creating and marketing a memorabilia, and art print business, you may not experience the same results, hopefully better. Perhaps the most valuable information from this book is the thought process I went through to get my products created and sold.

My hope for you is that you will create a memorabilia business by having fun with the process.

Memorabilia Madness

Memorabilia Madness

What is the memorabilia business?

Memorabilia for the purpose of this book is defined as a noun which means objects valued for their connection with historical events, culture, or entertainment: posters, publicity photographs, and products. (The free dictionary) I used this definition when gathering the images needed to produce the products for my business. I learned that when collecting images for my products that many of the images would work well for art prints also. In this book I cover not only making products for the memorabilia business but also making prints for the art market.

Wide variety of products

The memorabilia business is an enormous industry. According to the Greeting Card Association there were 6.5 billion cards sold last year with sales between 7 and 8 billion dollars. This figure is just for greeting cards and does not include the plethora of other memorabilia.

The New York Times reported that in the sixty days leading up to Christmas; E-Bay reported 13,137 handmade items were sold at an average price of $8.21. Not all of these products are memorabilia, but many of them are.

The size of the industry presents a good news bad news situation. The good news is there many items to choose from. The bad news you have to choose which ones will be profitable for your business. New trends, colors, and styles are always changing. The list you create today needs to evolve.

Which products should I sell?

My choice of what products to sell today may be different than my choice of products two or three years from now. How did I decide what products to sell? Believe me it is an ongoing process, but I did have to start somewhere.

My first step was to make a list of the products I liked, and thought I might be able to produce. I created this list of product from the top of my head. The list was in no particular order, and I gave no consideration to how to make the product or how profitable a product might be.

I compiled a list of products that I considered for my business at the time when I first began to create my memorabilia business. The list of products I considered are large prints, postcards, buttons, bumper stickers, greeting cards, key chains, posters, refrigerator magnets, book marks, books, and calendars.

Research

My second step was to use my list and begin researching the products I wish to sell. I took each product and created a scoring table for the products. The table consisted of five categories, ease to produce, cost to produce, selling price both wholesale and retail, distribution, and demand. Using one through ten I evaluated each product, in each category. Scoring a one for the easiest and least investments, to ten for the hardest and most costly investment, I set out to determine what products that I would create and sell. Now it is time to learn. Let's take a look at each of the categories.

Ease to produce

Is the product something I have the skill level to produce a quality product? Do I have the tools such as software and printers that can produce a quality product? Can a scale the product and make a profit from it. Some products are easy to produce once I have the machine to produce them. I have to ask myself, is it worth the investment in a machine to produce a product. I gave the easiest product to produce a low number, and the hardest a higher number. If I had to purchase a machine to make the product I assigned a number no lower than five.

Cost to produce

The answer to this question is fairly straight forward. My rating in this category came from how much money up front was required to produce the product and how much each product would cost. I also had to consider the impact of purchasing in bulk, and at what point is too many to buy at one time. I had very little to invest.

It is hard to nail down an exact cost on many products, so on my chart I tried to list a range of prices.

Selling Price

This question was twofold. First question, what would be the selling price based on the best cost I could come up with and is there any room left for profit? The second question I asked is will people be willing to pay the price I need to make a profit?

I encountered a similar problem with setting a selling price without a solid cost figure to base the price upon. I the case of my chart I estimated a range of possible selling prices. I based my selling estimate on my best guess of cost, and selling prices I have seen elsewhere.

Distribution

How will I get my product in front of the people that will purchase them? Will I need transportation? Will I need to purchase a machine to package my product, such as a laminator? Should I be wholesale only? Should I set minimum quantities? Will I need to purchase a bar code? If so how much will a bar code cost? How much additional packaging will I need? The answer to these questions can make the difference between a profit and a loss.

The biggest factor in my rating of distribution is the additional cost of packaging. I again used the one through ten number system, with one the easiest and ten the most difficult.

Demand

Real easy question, but very difficult to determine: Is there enough people that would want to buy my products to make such product worthwhile to produce.

How do I access demand? I look at what others are selling. I look at websites that sell the type of products I am selling and research what they are selling. Many sites also publish the search terms that people are searching for. I can look at how many are searching for what I sell and get a feel for what the demand is.

I have learned one of the biggest mistakes an entrepreneur can make is assuming there is a market for their product or service. Regardless of what I felt might be a strong product, I relied on the hard facts that I could find. Some products are tracked better than others, making the data easy to find. Some products I could find no data at all.

When the data and my feelings about a product come together, then I believe I have found a product that will sell.

The rating on my chart for this category is again one through ten. One is being no too little demand, and ten being high demand.

Conducting Research

I have determined the questions I need to answer, but how should I go about collecting data? My research took place in two different ways, in person visits, and online research. There is a copy of the chart I used for my research at the end of the book.

In person visits

Gifts shops

I never miss a chance to stop in and visit a gift shop. I love to look at the products that are being offered, and learn from them. I always watch what other patrons are buying. I look at the packaging, colors, display, and different price points. I look at the amount of space a particular product is given by the store.

When it is the off season and times are slow I sometimes will catch the owner working. This is a great time to ask questions from those that know. If I am not a competitor I find that most will freely talk about their business. You may even get so lucky that the owner will tell you he paid for certain products, terms, and how well they sell certain products. I may also learn of any products they would like to have but don't. This type of information can be the most valuable information you can have, and all it takes is a little conversation.

In this category I have also included visits to art galleries of all types. When I enter a gallery I try to take note of everything. Is the gallery clean, organized, inviting, and comfortable? What type of art work do they represent? Is the gallery a cop-op, individually, or corporate owned? Does the gallery take on new artist? Do they want exclusivity? Do they offer services like framing or printing?

Drug Stores

I research both large mass market drug and independent drug stores. A visit to a drug store can be a good source to learn about greeting cards (notice the amount of space given), and novelty products that will sell. Many times you can ascertain the top sellers by the lack of inventory of the product. Most of the large chain stores will not even sell a product if it doesn't sell well.

Other retail outlets

This category includes all chain stores such as Wal-Mart and Target. This is also a category that contains grocery and convenience stores. If I see a product that I want to sell at one of these mass market stores, then I can assume that the product will be a good selling product. I have found postcards at many convenience stores, and when asked the clerk if they sell, I was told they sell very well.

Online

When I first started in the memorabilia business there was very little information available anywhere. This is certainly not the case anymore. The internet provides a ton of information on all the aspects of this type of business, and continues to grow. The biggest issue with searching for information via the net is overload. There is just too much information to comprehend, and I haven't even mentioned selling online.

I found that most of the research ended up in four types of categories. These categories are greeting card companies, industry news, other people's work, and vendor sites.

Greeting Card companies

It only makes sense that if you interested in this type of a market to check out the big guys. When searching drill down a few pages and investigate some of the smaller companies. Be sure to look at the submission guidelines for all the companies you search. You may find that providing images or verse for these companies is better for you then creating and producing your own card line.

Just as in personal visits I am sure to look at design, colors, and verse for inspiration. I notice how many cards now have embellishments, and the higher price this type of card brings. I was sure in the learning process that I examined invitations and boxed sets of cards.

Industry news

I found a great way to start and learn about the memorabilia industry is to locate news groups that follow what I am learning about. This may require that I follow different groups for different types of products. There are organizations that are devoted to the greeting card industry, photo novelties, and fine art just to mention a few.

There is much to be learned from these groups and will also keep you up on all the trends in the business. Several times I have found that information on the new colors for the season can help get a heads up on design.

While I am on the subject of groups, I should mention that user groups are also very valuable source of information, inspiration, and guidance. These groups are easy to locate on social sites like Facebook, LinkedIn, Twitter, and other social sites. Joining one of the groups can help answer questions and develop ideas for a profitable memorabilia business. Some of these groups can be very specialized and I may need to join more than one type of group to obtain all the information I need.

Other people's work

Looking for and viewing other people's work can be a lot of fun, inspirational, and very time consuming. Most creative people look at the design or perhaps the site itself, but what you I am looking at is how I found the site in the first place. Was it through a search engine? Was it through one of the groups I joined? What search words did I use? These are all things that I should be looking into when I visit the site of others I have found.

Vendor's Websites

I would say that half the information I needed to start my memorabilia business came from vendors' websites. Vendors have a lot to gain by sharing information about their area of the industry. Many vendors offer a person to answer any questions I may have, which is a great service when needed.

Vendor websites were also very helpful in setting prices. Without their help it would be very difficult to establish the cost of products. For example, Red River Paper will tell you how much it cost to print a single greeting card based on printer, paper, and ink combination. This is a very helpful feature of the site. The end of this book includes links to the vendors I used.

Results of Research

I tried not to make any judgments, just collect the facts, about a product during the research process, but now it is time to evaluate each product as an item I can produce, market, and sell at a profit. What follows are my thoughts on the products.

Prints

There is a market for prints of all types. Framed and ready to hang prints will out sell just loose or matted prints. Making prints for the memorabilia market allows you to be a creative as you can possibly be. Prints may be as simple as ink on paper rolled up in a tube, matted and framed, or printed on another substrate like aluminum.

I currently have everything needed to enter the print market and would have to invest very little. There seem to be many outlets to market my prints to. Framed and ready prints seem to have a high perceived value, which can lead to nice profits.

Many vendors offer a service that will print, frame, and ship my prints directly to my clients. This is a wonderful feature, which can save me money and hassle. Vendors list the price I pay for the product and allow me to set my own prices that the client pays.

Selling prints can allow me to be as creative as possible. There is no limit to the type of prints that I can create. I find selling prints very exciting.

Postcards

Almost everybody I know has purchased post cards at one time. The market for post cards is alive and strong. Post cards can be produced easily, and allow a great deal of creativity in design and images.

Very little money is involved in making postcards. Printing is the biggest expense, and I can find a wide variation of prices based on quantity and size. I found that the most popular size is around 4.25 inches by 6 inches.

Post cards have a strong following. There are collectors and clubs devoted to the collecting of post cards. There are sites on the internet that encourages people to share and send postcards from all over the world.

Greeting Cards

Greeting cards are a second cousin to prints and post-cards. Many now consider a handmade card as an expensive gift. Greeting cards are easy to produce, and allow a great deal of freedom in design, images, and writing.

Printing is also the biggest expense with greeting cards, and there are three methods of having my cards printed. Method number one is to print them myself.

The second method would be to have a printing company print them for you. The third method is a variation of having someone prints them for you, and that is a print on demand service. There are many of these services available on the internet. At the end of the book is a list of some of the companies I have used.

Greeting cards can have a low profit margin, but volume can sometimes make up for the low margin. Greeting cards have several methods of packaging that help increase volume. Cards can sold one at a time or boxed and sold as sets. The added asset of having several packaging options increases creativity, design, and can allow for "themes" in marketing.

Posters

Posters are a little tricky to sell. Those that sell posters are able to do so due to volume printing, which allows a price reasonable enough to sell the poster. Printing cost is the most prohibitive reason to entering the poster market. To have enough posters printed to keep the price low enough to make a profit requires a rather large investment. Design of a poster can be from simple to a complex composite. There is a great deal of freedom with creativity in design, and images.

Books

E-books have definitely had an effect on the sale of printed books, but printed books are still alive and selling well. There is a learning curve with producing your own books, but it is possible to have total control over the creative process. The most enticing part of writing and publishing books is the low or no cost option of publishing. With my money so tight publishing books may be the best profit for the amount of money invested.

Wrapping Paper

Everybody uses wrapping paper. Wrapping paper is easy to create with the use of Photoshop tools. The way to sell wrapping paper is to sell one of my designs to a company that prints wrapping paper.

Magnets

Refrigerator magnets can be a good seller. Almost every house I go in there are magnets on their refrigerator. Magnets are easy to create and off a wide range in freedom with your images. Magnets are easy to have printed and will not cost an arm and a leg.

Key Chains

Key chains can be handmade or printed by a printing company. Design is easy and there is wide latitude in the images you can use. There is also a wide assortment of the types of key chains available. There are internet companies that offer easy design, production, and help in selling key chains.

Calendars

Calendars require at least 13 images to produce. There is a very short selling period for calendars, and printing cost may be too high to make a profit selling single calendars. I can market my calendars to businesses as promotional gifts and increase volume. Designing calendars can be a lot of fun and allow for the use of themes.

Bumper Stickers

Bumper stickers are easy to design, and can be printed at home. Profit per item is very good, but bumper sticker can be low volume sellers. This is an item that can also be produced with some of the online companies.

Other photo novelties

This is an ever changing category of products. This category contains items such as but not limited to, mugs, plates, tote bags, snow globes, jewelry, and T-shirts. Some of these items are easy to design, especially if you use some of the online tools that are available.

Worksheet on Product Research

Product	Ease to Produce	Cost to produce	Selling Price	Demand	Distribution
Framed prints	2	$18-99	$25-500	3	8
Matted prints	1	12-99	25-75	2	8
Buttons	5	$.5-1.	1.5-3.00	4	5
Posters	8	$2.00 +	10.00	3	2
Post Cards	2	$.12	$.35	6	5
Greeting Cards	3	1.00	2.75 +	3	3
Calendars	8	4.00 +	7.5+	2	4
Books	8	0- 5.00+	.99-45.00	8	5
Magnets	1	.25+	1.00+	2	5
Key chains	2	.75+	1.50+	2	5
Mouse Pads	1	1.75+	6.00+	1	5
Bumper Stickers	3	$1.00	$2.00	2	5

Many of the products that I have discussed can be designed, produce, and sold through on of the internet companies that I have listed at the end of the book. Even if I do not use any of these companies I still visit the sites to see what's new.

Too Many products

Through my research I discovered there are hundreds of products to offer to your customers. My research was on over a dozen products, and several E-commerce sites that would allow me even more options. I took my list and the research and I did something real simple; I picked the products that interested me the most.

Make a list of the products you want to produce and sell

With my table from my research I determined which products I wanted to produce, promote, and sell. This list ended up being quite long, and I had to narrow the list of products down to just a few. I was working with very little money, so I needed the biggest bag for my investment. Now, this is where the chart from research really helped determine the final list of products. Using my chart and intuition I was able to narrow the list of products I wanted to produce.

Create Your Final List

I finalized my list with these five products, framed prints, matted prints, buttons, post cards, and greeting cards. Sure there were other products that I would like to create, but I needed to stick with those that I felt would make me the most money.

Memorabilia Madness

Memorabilia Madness

Create Your Products

Now that I know what product I want to create and sell, it is time to start the process, and get the ball rolling. This is a crucial part of the process; you have to idea of what the final product will look like. My research gave me the information, and ideas of what my products should look like. Knowing the products I want to produce, and an idea of how they should look, I got down to business.

This is the fun part

Creating my products is a lot of fun. I have chosen products that require great images. I need many images in fact. As you can tell I am a list maker, and so it is with the images that are needed to create products.

Where Do I find Images to Capture?

Images for my memorabilia and print business are all around me. Many times I do not have to travel more than ten feet from my front door. When I first started this business I was always looking for the next spectacular photo, only to miss the one in front of my nose.

Stay Local

My recent trip to Yellowstone National Park is of very little use to me in my southern rural town. I have learned that people buy memorabilia because of an emotional attachment to a particular location. Since my market was local then my images need to be local. How do I determine what's of value locally? Easy answer: Ask. Ask my neighbors, visitors, and anyone that has a favorite location or memory.

Learn the Local History

History is being made every day. Research and locate where historical events have taken place, and set out to capture the scene. Visit the locations many times and try to convey the emotion of the times. I try to limit the radius of historical events to about fifty miles from my home town.

City and State, Parks and Gardens

Many times it is at a park that childhood memories are made. Locations like this can be a source of many wonderful images. When I photograph in these locations I try to keep in mind that many have an emotional attachment to a location. People buy because of emotion, so the more emotion I can convey in my photographs the better chance I have of making the sell.

Parks and gardens are easy to locate. I cannot think of a town that I have visited that did not have a park of some kind. State websites list state parks and include hours of operation, fees, and types of facilities that are provided. Most locations have websites that help in planning a photo excursion, such as wild flower blooming periods, bird migration, water levels, and more.

My Front Yard garden

There are never enough images from the garden. I have used and continue to use hundreds of images from my garden. The garden changes every day. It is easy to create beautiful greeting cards with stellar images from the garden.

To make selling floral images easier I make sure to keep all the names of plants that I plant. Many times the material that comes with the plants or seeds includes the Latin name for the species. Having this information can make a searching for particular images much easier. I use Adobe Lightroom for importing and cataloging my images and include this data in my saved images.

With my list of possible landmarks, I took to the streets, gardens, and parks to capture my images.

Collect Images

I have now been collecting images for over fifteen years. It is an ongoing process, and I enjoy it tremendously. You would think with over fifteen years, and thousands of images I would have all I need. There are still Landmarks on the list that I have not yet been able to create anything that I could use as one of my products.

Create designs

To create the designs, and handle files I used Adobe Creative Suite 5. There is quite a bit of a learning curve with the Adobe products, and if you are not already a user then you might consider using another software provider. There are many online design tools that are easy to use, and can do the job. However I decide to design my products a properly prepared image and saved in the correct format can make the difference between a mediocre product and a great product.

It is at this point that I needed to stop and learn about color management. To have my images appear as the printed products I created look like the images I created on my monitor I learned about color space. A through description of color management is beyond the scope of this book, however I urge anyone wanting to create printed products of any kind learn about color management. There are many good resources on the net, and at the book store.

I also should mention that I needed to learn about file formats. I was already familiar with JPEG and TIFF formats but there are many more that I needed to learn about. My biggest piece of advice when it comes to dealing with file formats is to know what kind of file your finial output needs to be to produce your product.

Most of what I create is produced using Adobe Creative Suite. Adobe creative suite has a very time consuming learning curve, and may not be the choice of software for everyone. There are many other software companies that I have looked into, but chose to stay with Adobe products.

I still relied on some other software to help with starting and running my business. I used Microsoft Office for all my word processing. There are many companies that offer words processing software, but I choose to go with Office because it seemed to be the standard. Most computers can read a word document. Word is the name of the word processing module in MS office and will integrate with very important accounting software to run my business.

One of the most important software programs is QuickBooks. QuickBooks has nothing to with design or creating products but is must if I am to keep track of my business. This is a business and must be treated as such. QuickBooks has excellent tools for managing my business. There is also a feature that will allow me to use my QuickBooks customer list in a Word document. I can send personalized material to customers, vendors, and contractors. The integration between Word and Quick-Books is a wonderful aid in marketing.

QuickBooks is not the only software available to keep track of my business, but I have found it to be very easy to use, and very helpful in running my business. I could not think of starting and running a business without some type of accounting software.

Test

I have several of plastic containers filled with products that never made it past this stage of development. I used an informal method of testing my products. I showed my product to everyone I could find and asked them what they thought of the product. If their answer was a positive response, I then asked if they would be willing to purchase the product. My next question was to ask if they would be willing to pay the price I had hoped to sell for.

My method of testing is certainly not scientific or statistically correct, but I did learn some good information both positive and negative. I learned to listen and make changes that I did not always agree with. I learned that what was my favorite was not always the choice of my customers. The key issue is that I was able to take comments from others and adapt my products for better sales.

I have now created my product, tested it, and have made the decision to offer it for sale. I take a moment to relax and celebrate my success; I've come a long way since I have decided to follow this path. The items that I choose to create and sell are

- Prints of all types

- Postcards of local landmarks

- Greeting cards of all types

- Buttons

- Key chains

- Bumper stickers

    The question I have to ask myself now is: who will buy my product? It is now time to market the hard and fun work I have done so far.

Memorabilia Madness

Marketing your products

There are hundreds if not thousands of books on marketing. There are books on marketing greeting cards, and fine art. There is good chance that there is a book written on the same idea you have. At the end of this book is a list of the resources that I have used which includes some of the books I learned from. What I try to explain in this section of the book are the ideas I used and explored to sell my products. There is not any guarantee that any of my methods will work for you, but you can still learn from what I have done.

Some Decisions to make

The first things I learned are, I needed a plan to implement. Before I could create my plan I needed to ask myself some questions. Who provides display? Should I sell wholesale or retail? How should I handle returns? How much cash do I have to spend? Do I have the skills to market my products? How much time do I need to allocate for marketing? I had to take some time to think about answers to these questions.

I found that when answering these questions that each individual product had its' own marketing challenges. For example, I did not market postcards the same as I did floral prints. So let's continue with the process; wholesale or retail?

Wholesale

The definition of wholesale is to sale goods in large

quantities for resale. I was a wholesale floral distributor for over thirty years and I am very familiar with the plusses and minuses of the wholesale business. All the products I am offering can be sold on a wholesale level, but I believed that postcards, buttons and greeting cards could be best sold through wholesale methods.

The plus side of doing business on a wholesale level is less people to deal with and larger orders. The best part of selling wholesale is that the client already has costumers ready to buy.

The negative side of selling wholesale is I have to invest more money upfront, possibly have to carry receivables, and I may have to provide bar codes.

Bottom line on selling wholesale is that there is more cash required up front to make a sell, but having retailers sell my products for me is worth the cash investment.

Retail

There are some products that I believe that are difficult to sale on a wholesale level. Fine art prints fall in to this category. Each print sale in unique and most of the time requires a conversation between the photographer and the buyer. On the flip side, I would go crazy trying to sell postcards one at a time. Selling retail requires a different marketing approach then selling wholesale.

Packaging

Packaging a product is just as important as the product itself. There are several things I needed to consider. Do I sell greeting cards one at a time or do a sell many cards in a boxed set? How should I package framed prints? How much is all this packaging going to cost me?

I had to take each of my products and answer the packaging questions. I studied the way others had packaged similar products. I searched the internet for answers and between the two I developed a packaging system for my products.

Postcards are sold in bulk and did not require any kind of packaging. Greeting cards are sold in boxed sets of eight cards with envelopes and individually. Individual greeting cards are packaged in a clear bag. Buttons are mounted two buttons on a cardboard card and then placed in the same size and type bag as the greeting cards. Bumper stickers and key chains are also mounted on a cardboard card and placed in the same clear bag as the other prod-

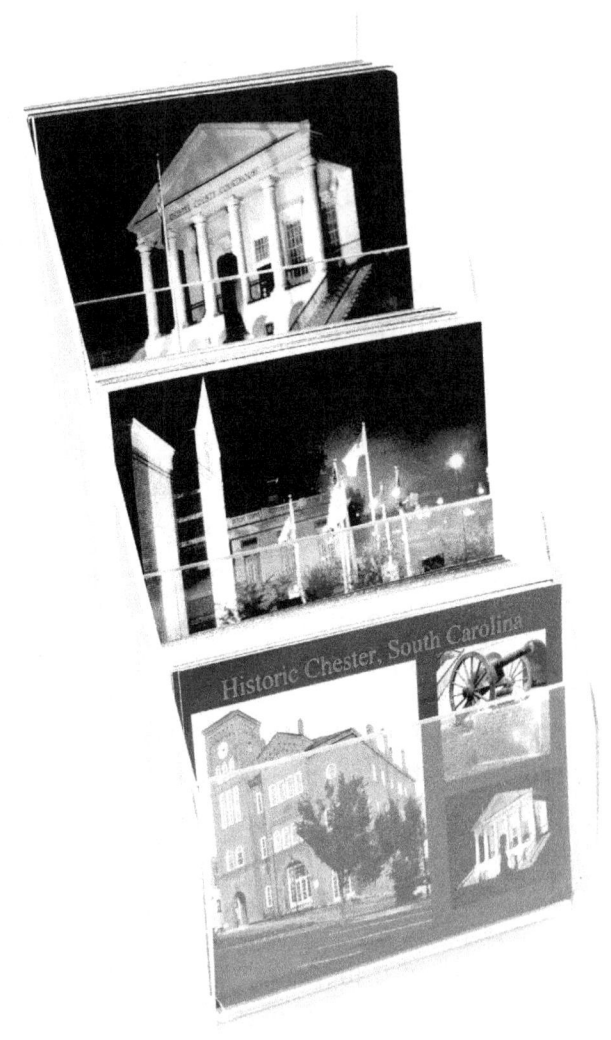

Three tier counter top postcard display

same services other vendors do.

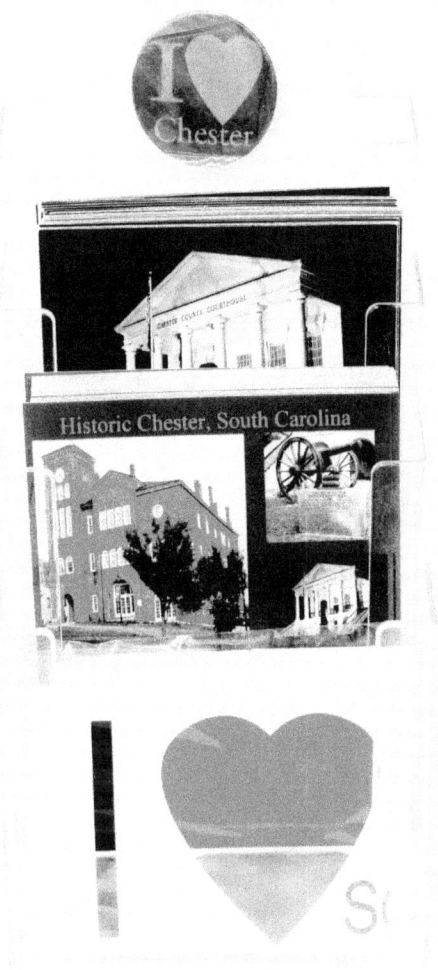

Four tier counter top display. This one contains 2 postcards, bumper sticker, and buttons.

There are as many different types of display fixtures as there are products. Prices on fixtures vary widely also. Search many vendors and you will discover that quantity talks. The purchase of several free standing floor racks can easily be hundreds of dollars. This decision needs to be made before I can establish prices and a marketing plan.

With my packaging in mind I choose to stick with display stands that were made for postcards and greeting cards. This type of display gave me many options. Postcard and greeting card stands and counter top displays can range from a three tier counter top display to a six foot free standing floor display with 25 pockets.

The resource section of this book lists some of the companies I used.

Memorabilia Madness

Establish my prices

With the decision to sell both wholesale and retail it was time to establish prices. Setting prices can always be a tricky situation. Everyone wants to make as much profit as possible, but too high a price and you scare people away. I also have the dilemma of setting prices for wholesale customers and prices for my retail customers. Let's start with wholesale pricing first.

Pricing for wholesale

There is no magic formula that I have to set my prices. Many times establishing the price for my products is an ongoing trial and error process. The best method I have learned to price products is to use my "base cost" and research from earlier of products similar to mine. My "base cost" is the amount of money it takes to produce the item. This cost does not include any time spent of the item. For example it cost me around a twenty cents per postcard in short run quantities delivered. Twenty cents a card is my "base Cost." My research will give me an idea of where to start my pricing.

Many believe that I should include all the cost it takes to produce a product, such as time spent on capture, editing, and research. I feel that these are impossible at start up to calculate. It may take an hour for capture, and another for editing, but if I end up selling ten thousand post cards for the images captured, the cost is very little. If from the same shot I end up selling only ten cards, then the cost is quite high. I have learned to sick with my physical costs and just keep making images that might sell.

One other cost under the term of display is the cost to package the item. These include plastic bags or shrink wrap, tags, and labels. The individual per item cost may not be but a few pennies, but the amount can add up fast. I failed to add this cost into my calculations until I received my first one thousand bags and the bill was over a hundred dollars.

With my per unit "base cost" and my display cost I can set my prices. With my cost and prices determined I can begin to package and market my business. The following chart is my wholesale price list for the year 2013

Notice I do not list the prices of the packages as individual items. Prices are for everything including the display stand. At the bottom I list the recommend retail price but do not insist that the products be sold for that amount. Each store has their own pricing formula, and it is best to let the seller determine their selling price.

Sample certifacate of aunthenicity

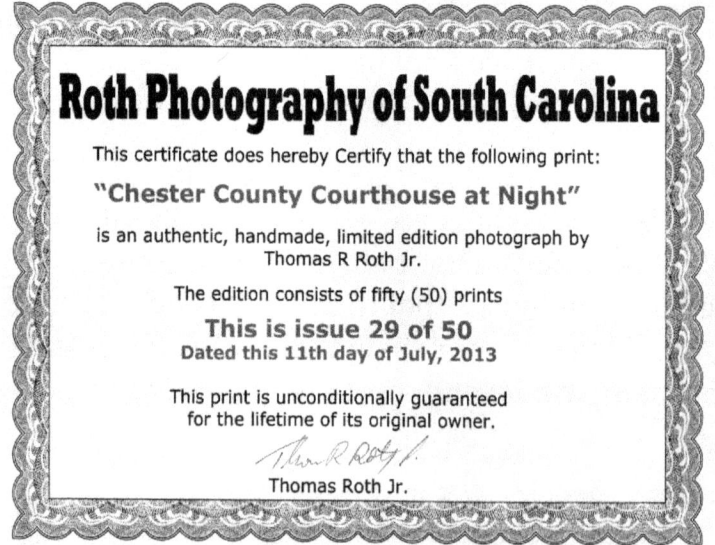

Roth Photography of South Carolina

This certificate does hereby Certify that the following print:

"Chester County Courthouse at Night"

is an authentic, handmade, limited edition photograph by
Thomas R Roth Jr.

The edition consists of fifty (50) prints

This is issue 29 of 50
Dated this 11th day of July, 2013

This print is unconditionally guaranteed
for the lifetime of its original owner.

Thomas Roth Jr.

My wholesale Price List

Chester-Gifts

Product Display and Inventory

Counter Top Spinner

Measurements- 9" Diameter Base, 18" High

$604.60

840	Postcards	12 different designs
80	I ♥ Chester Bumper Stickers	1 per package
30	I ♥ Chester Buttons	2 per package
20	I ♥ Chester Key Tags	1 per package

Free standing Floor Spinner

Measurements- 66" High

$796.60

1140	Postcards	21 different designs
120	I ♥ Chester Bumper Stickers	1 per package
50	I ♥ Chester Buttons	2 per package
40	I ♥ Chester Key Tags	1 per package

Memorabilia Madness

Four Tier Product Counter Display

Measurements- 6.5" High, 10" High

$82.80

50	Postcards	Single Design
20	I ♥ Chester Bumper Stickers	1 per package
10	I ♥ Chester Buttons	2 per package
7	I ♥ Chester Key Tags	1 per package

Three Tier Postcard Only Counter Display

Measurements- 6.75" Wide, 10.5" High

$81.60

225	Postcards	3 different designs

Product Prices-Wholesale

Item	Cost	Suggested Retail price
Buttons 2per package	$2.20	$ 3.00
Key Chains	1.90	3.00
Postcards	.39	.75
Bumper Stickers	1.50	2.50

149 Wylie St Chester SC 29706▪ 803.385.2514 ▪ thomas@chester-gifts.com

Memorabilia Madness

Pricing Retail

When it comes to pricing for my retail customers my number one rule is; never sell below what my wholesale customers are selling my product for. Never! With this rule in mind, I have one group of products left to price, and that is art prints.

Selling prints is different from selling memorabilia products. True many of the images that I used in making my memorabilia products were also art prints on high quality paper, their audiences are vastly different. The sales outlets for prints are galleries and direct to the public.

Selling direct to the public requires some type of venue to display my work. I have learned that I can sell prints from such places as banks, restaurants, hospitals, and beauty salons. There is no limit to the businesses that I can display my work in if I just use some imagination. Dealing with galleries and with the public can present pricing issues.

The largest cost with selling prints that I have encountered is the cost to market them. Producing the product is not what eats up your budget but, getting the word out is. If I consign my prints to a gallery the commission is very often around fifty percent. If I direct my marketing efforts to the public with advertising the cost per sale may well exceed fifty percent. I tried both methods, and both were successful.

So, how did I end up pricing my art prints? I priced them to sell at galleries. I believe that offering my prints at a gallery increases the perceived value of the print: therefore I was able to price the prints for a nice profit per print.

While I am one the subject of profit per print it is a good time to mention the issue of "limited edition" or "open edition" prints. My quick definition of "limited edition prints" and "open edition prints" is simple: If I sell a limited edition print then, once I have reached the limit I cannot sell any more. There can many variables to limited edition prints. Variables such as print size, substrate, and paper options can be included as part of the edition or spate from the editions. I have offered both types of editions, and I have far more successful selling "limited edition "prints. The customer enjoys the fact that they are purchasing a prints that will not be available everywhere.

To make my limited edition prints seem more valuable to the customer I include a *certificate of authenticity*. A *certificate of authenticity (COA)* is a document that states title, creation date, artist, total number in the edition, and the edition number of that individual print. Along with the COA I sign each print and include the edition as print number (Example 20) over the total number in the edition (example 50) 20/50 ma search on the internet has provided me with plenty of samples to derive my COA. I have included a sample of my COA in resource section.

I have now have chosen my display fixtures, created, produced, packaged and priced my products. It's time to sell, and of course everyone wants my products so I'll just sit back and fill the orders. Great plan, just one small problem: no one knows who I am and what I have to offer. Worse yet, I don't know who they are and what to offer them.

Identify your customers

It is time now to begin identifying potential customers. I am looking for retail establishments to sell my product, galleries, businesses, and individuals to buy prints.

Build Lists

The use of a good database became invaluable in this process. As I entered each prospect into the database I would code each to be used in the sorting process. I had four different codes.

First code was for prospects that would only be interested in reselling my products. Many businesses that sell to the public fit into this code.

My second code was prospects that would be interested in purchasing my prints. Establishments like doctor's offices, hospitals, executive's offices, and attorney's offices.

Third code was for galleries.

Fourth code was for prospects that would be interested in purchasing prints, and reselling my products.

Identifying clients for wholesale

To build my list of potential clients that would be interested in selling my products or buying my prints, I turned to the trusted phone book. I am sure there many ways to build lists through the internet, and it is easy to buy a list of potential clients. I used the yellow pages and a database program to build a list of potential clients, this worked well for me.

I did not limit myself to just the use of the phone book, I also added all contacts through personal connections. I collect business cards from everyone I meet and make sure I add them to the database.

Identifying Customers for Retail

Creating a list of clients to sell my art prints was very easy. I just made a list of all the places I wanted to see my prints hanging in. My list included medical offices, attorneys' offices, bank lobbies, restaurants, and the walls of some executives. All the businesses that I needed to contact were in the same zip code, which helps keep delivery cost to a minimum.

When creating my list I try to find the name of the person who has the power to buy my products. In many cases this person would be the owner, and an important contact for future projects. Of course having their name gave my direct mail a personal touch.

Summary on Finding Clients

Obtaining clients for any business can be difficult endeavor. The best client is the one you already have. I cherish every client that I have. I always try to send each of my clients' thank you cards for their purchase. I know that in order for my business to grow I must NEVER stop looking for new clients, and NEVER take my current clients for granted.

Choose your method of contact

Contacting and engaging potential clients is a huge subject, and beyond the scope of this book. There are thousands of resources available. I cannot stress enough to read the Guerrilla Marketing books by Jay Conrad Levinson. There is a plethora of ideas that anyone can implement for very little investment. I cannot also stress enough to have multiple methods of promoting your products. Here are some of the methods I use.

Internet marketing

Internet marketing is another subject that hundreds of books have as their subject. My current internet marketing uses mostly free sites to promote my products. As of this writing I have nine different sites working for me. Each site has a specific audience and is tailored to them. All of the sites that I use are free to set-up and promote; however some of the sites do take a commission.

All of my activity is geared to direct viewers to one of my sites. The activity I am referring to is the use of social media. I use Facebook, LinkedIn, and Google + to attract people that are looking for the products I sell. I post links to everything I do on the web.

I also use Google alerts to follow blogs and articles that may have a similar type audience that I am selling to. When a blog post or something similar that I can comment on, I do so. I always try to include a link to one of the websites. This method of marketing does not cost any money, but can take some time to cultivate.

I have created several Facebook pages for my business. I have also began using Google+, and twitter to promote my products. I have recently begun to use company such as Hubspot to bring all my social activity into one place.

I have also purchased ads on Yahoo, Google, and Bing. I have found that these ads can drive traffic to your sites but, that does not always convert into sales. What I have gotten from running ads is an email mailing list of possible clients. This email list is a great resource mostly because the people that have signed up are already interested in what I am selling. These lists have produced sales.

Non-internet marketing

The internet is not the only method to market my products. Before the web, direct mail, television, radio, magazines, and newspapers were the methods used to get the word out about my products. All of these methods require some type of financial investment. I discovered that direct mail gave me the best value for the investment.

I marketed my art prints directly to businesses with the use of postcards. I created four different postcard mailers. Each postcard offered the same set of three limited edition framed prints. I printed the cards at my office on five by seven card stock. I used the list of businesses that I had compiled earlier and timed the mailing to be about five days apart. My results were an astounding thirty percent response, and resulted in sales of all but a couple of a fifty print limited edition

You may ask why I choose to offer my prints as a limited edition. My answer is quite simple: the customer perceives a higher value to a limited edition print than an open edition. I currently have both open editions and limited edition prints for sale. I have by far made more money selling limited edition prints.

My last word on art prints is when I made a sell, and it was time for delivery, I would personally deliver the framed prints with white cotton gloves on. It never hurts to show my clients that I care deeply about the product they have bought. I do not want to deliver a print that has fresh new finger prints on it. I think that the gloves add that little something extra that shows I am a professional.

Memorabilia Madness

Merge the physical with the internet

On everything I create I put information about my company. I put my physical address and phone number on all my paper products. To merge the physical with the information highway is use QR codes.

QR codes are black and white squares that are like bar codes. QR stands for quick response, and was invented by Toyota in 1994. I cannot recommend enough to use QR codes on as many products as possible. If I cannot put the code on the product itself, such as the back of greeting cards, then I put the code somewhere on the packaging. The QR code uses smart phone technology to direct the customer to my Missing Toe Publishing web site. Below is a copy of the QR code to link to my site.

Make the sale

No matter what method I use to contact potential customers it almost always comes down to making the sale on a face to face basis. My advice to anyone who wants to sell their products is to learn how to sell. Business Guru Brain Moran says it better than I can: Unless your product is so revolutionary that people are willing to line up at your door for it, you need to learn how to sell; otherwise, your days as a business owner are numbered."

Many people believe that I must have a website in order to participate in web activities. I found that the only thing I need to participate on the web is an e-mail address. I have had my e-mail address for over fifteen years and it is the only thing that has not changed since I have been participating on the web. A website is optional, but to have a site is a good idea. I have found success in using free site that are easy to set up and use.

I believe that as a photographer a website is a must if I want people to see what I can do. Using free sites that are available such as Yola, or Webs, I can test my site for free, and if I need more then I can purchase the upgrade. Free sites and their easy to use set up tools can give me a website that can be used to promote myself. But, I do not just want to promote myself; I want to sell my products. I want to make money!

Internet Store Fronts

I have made mention of the internet several times in research and marketing but I would like to take some time and explore internet store fronts available. There are many sites that are available to anyone that would like to create and sell memorabilia and art prints, and I participate in several.

Selling Prints on the Internet

Selling prints on the internet is becoming a huge business and has many players. To narrow sites that I would be interested in I had to determine that the site promoted what I was selling. I did not want to sell portrait packages or wedding albums. I wanted to sell prints that people wanted to hang on their walls art. I use Fine Art America.

Fine Art America has a free version and a paid version. The free version is wonderful and only gets better with the paid version. From the Fine Art America site I can sell quality prints in several different print surfaces. I can also sell greeting cards of the images I place on the site. I can set the amount of profit I want to make on each item for sell. They also offer professional framing if the customer desires to purchase a ready to hang product. Fine Art America handles all the printing, collection of payment, and delivery. Fine Art America works for me as a way to offer high quality prints to everyone.

Selling Memorabilia on the Internet

I use Zazzle.com for memorabilia products. It seems the list of available products that I can customize with my images and words are endless. Zazzle.com handles all the production, collecting and delivery for me. Zazzle allows me to sell products that I cannot afford to make large investments in. There are several companies that offer stores to sell memorabilia products through. Many people I have found like to do business with Café Press. I must recommend that anyone interested in this type of business should take their time and explore all of the options that are available.

Selling Greeting cards on the Internet

Greeting Card Universe (GCU) is a company that only sells greeting cards. At the time of this writing they offer the customer to order a card online and then pick up the card at their local Target store. The profit on cards sold through the GCU store is very small and may be a bit discouraging. GCU handles all of the work. They print, mail, and collect the payment. GCU pays out once per quarter.

Several of the sites I explored allowed me to sell greeting cards, but I have had the most success with GCU. Fine Art America also allows me to offer greeting cards of the images that I have on display with them.

As my collection of images grows I offer the best of the best available for download. I use Photoshelter for this type of sell. Photoshelter has a free start up version but to make full use of all the tools they offer I need to participate in one of their paid plans. Photoshelter also gives me a place to store hi resolution files and a method to sell them as a download.

Summary of Internet Store Fronts

Having a reputable company fulfill my orders is a nice feature of many of the internet store fronts. Collection of payments is another nice feature of doing business with an internet company. There are many positives of doing business with internet companies, I just had to take some time and find the correct company for me.

Store fronts on the internet do not guarantee customers. The sites that I have reviewed do advertise their services, and this creates a lot of traffic to the site. Lots of traffic to the site doesn't mean they are looking for me, but at least I have a chance to make a sell. I still have to market my products to the right group of prospects. Having an internet store front does give me options on selling my products.

What has worked for me?

I have enjoyed the last ten or so years I have been working on this project. I am not wealthy from selling memorabilia and prints, but that was never the reason to pursue this type of work.

I have learned that what I thought would be a sure top selling product was not. Images that I thought were just mediocre seemed to sell very well. I learned that I have to test everything again and again. I learned that peoples taste change and that my product line has to change also.

I learned that direct mail seemed to produce the best results so far, but I believe that social media will take over as the best marketing for the money. I will continue to test both methods and adapt.

I have learned that money is not always the issue with selling my products. Many of the retail clients are more afraid that their investment in my products will not sell. I try to remedy that issue by offering as many guarantees as possible. If I do not believe in my product's selling ability then why would my client care.

Most of all, I learned that nothing will happen if I don't make it happen.

Future of the industry

I believe that the memorabilia and print market will continue to grow. The transit it society that we live in will continue to produce new customers for my products. I believe that new channels to sell my products will continue to grow also. E-commerce is just beginning to make an impact on the buying public, and presents wonderful opportunities to create and sell more products.

I believe that there are many small markets such as mine that will fuel the growth in memorabilia products. The older American population becomes the more need there will be for products that bring found memories, and that is what the memorabilia business is all about.

I believe that the art print market will always be a hard market to make a profit, but there is plenty of room for creative and persistent entrepreneur. On line galleries will become the norm for most people buying art. A strong on line presence will determine who gets to show their work in the nations galleries.

Conclusion

Creating and marketing memorabilia and art products is not the easiest business to be in, but can be a lot of fun and very rewarding. What it takes to succeed in this business is hard work, thought into what people want to buy, and the guts to ask for the business.

Resources

The resources I have listed below are companies that I have done business with and books that I have read, and recommend.

Greeting Cards

Greeting Card Association. This can be a valuable resource on facts, trends, colors, pricing, and design about the greeting card industry. I cannot recommend enough to visit and learn from this site.

http://www.greetingcard.org/AbouttheIndustry/tabid/58/Default.aspx

Greeting Card Universe. GCU provides everything I need to have an online greeting card store. Easy to upload and create cards, Greeting Card Universe provides a store front and handles all sales, printing, and delivery of my cards. A feature that is unique to GCU at this time is the customer can choose to pick up their cards at their local Target store.

http://www.greetingcarduniverse.com

Card Maker Magazine- This is a magazine that is devoted to handmade cards. This is another good resource on trends, embellishments, and pricing of greeting cards.

http://www.cardmakermagazine.com

Stockwell Greetings-A longtime producer of greeting cards.

http://www.stockwellgreetings.com

Photographer's Edge- A great company to deal with. Their catalog is an inspiration to look at. Their products allow me to test ideas without a huge investment.

http://www.photographersedge.com/catalog.asp

Kate Harper's Blog- A good resource for advice on the greeting card business.

http://kateharperblog.blogspot.com/2009/05/10-card-publishers-artist-and-writer.html

48 Hour Books

https://www.48hrbooks.com

Jakprints

http://www.jakprints.com

Vistaprint. –I have used this company for short run post-cards, and calendars. This company has allowed me to test many products for very little investment.

www.vistaprints.com

QLT.com – QLT is a great resource for photo novelties such as key chains, snow globes, mouse pads, and tons more products.

www.qlt.com

Badge a Minit- This is the place for buttons. They offer turnkey solutions for anyone wanting to make their own buttons for around $30.00 at the time of this writing.

http://www.badgeaminit.com/

Red River Paper- Red River paper is the source for print yourself greeting cards. They offer a wide selection of paper choices and will even supply with envelopes and boxes. A useful feature of the site is the cost to print a card chart. I could use the chart to help with pricing my products.

www.redrierpaper.com

Display and Packaging.

U-Line – This is a site that has just about anything I will ever need to package and ship my products. They have very good customer service.

http://www.uline.com/index. aspx?pricode=WK621&utm_source=Bing&utm_ medium=cpc&utm_term=uline&utm_campaign=ULINE& gclid=CJD6oYXMmLgCFWWd7AodjxYAAA&gclsrc=ds

Argonaut Displays- This Company has a wide selection of display stands for postcards and greeting cards.

http://argonautpress.com/displays-post-card-racks.html

Crystal Clear Bags- If I need a clear bag, this is the place to start. http://www.clearbags.com/bags/clear-bags

Clear Display Solutions- This was a great resource for postcard displays and stands.

http://cleardisplays.com/

My Websites and Stores

Missing Toe Publishing

www.missingtoepublishing.webs.com

Exit-65

www.exit65thebook.webs.com

The dark side of Photography

www.thedarkside.webs.com

Chester Gifts Greeting Card Store

www.greetingcarduniverse.com/chestergifts

Roth photography web page on Photoshelter

http://rothphotosc.photoshelter.com/gallery/Images-of-South-Carolina/G0000RYvWJ4jPMCI/

Fine Art America- My store on Fine Art America

http://fineartamerica.com/profiles/rick-roth.html

Zazzle- My store front on Zazzle.

http://www.zazzle.com/chestergifts

Books

I have read over a thousand books on all subjects relating to the industry over the past fifteen years. Here are some my favorites.

Broit, Alan. Marketing Fine Art Photography. Santa Barbara, CA. Rocky Nook Inc. 2011--This is one of the best books I have ever read on the subject of marketing my photography. A must read.

Markle, Jamie. 2013 Photographer's Market. F+W Media, Inc. 2012--The name says it all. This book contains hundreds of places to sell my images. This is a great place to start looking for clients. I have kept my copies over the years in case I need to find a client from the past.

Zuckerman, Jim. Shooting and Selling your Photos. Writer's Digest Books, Cincinnati, Ohio 2003- This is a great resource about shooting and selling photos. Jim Zuckerman is a master at photography and selling. I found this book to be very useful in determining the direction of my images.

Weisgrau, Richard. Publishing Photography. Allenworth Press, New York NY 2006- This is a good resource for anyone pursuing the publishing market. Richard includes a section on "Finding Merchandise Clients", which is the memorabilia market.

Bourne, Scott. 88 Secrets. Olympic Mountain School Press, Gig Harbor, WA 2005- I find myself going back and reading this book over and over. Scott emphasizes the details that can make a difference in my business. Easy to read and written in common sense language.

Heller, Dan. Profitable Photography in the digital Age. Allworth Press, New York 2005- Dan Heller gives the facts about what it takes to succeed in the photography business. This is a very down to earth book with the cold hard facts about the business.

Sandman, Larry. A Guide to Greeting Card Writing. Writer Digest Books, Cincinnati, Ohio 1968- This is a good resource for anyone interested in writing verse for their greeting cards.

Engh, Ron Sellphotos.com. Writer Digest Books, Cincinnati, Ohio 2000- Ron Engh has written an excellent book on selling photography on the internet. This book is a great place to start. Visit the website for lots of information.

http://www.photosource.com/

Kawasaki, Guy Welch, Shawn. APE How to Publish a Book. Nononina Press USA. - Simply one of the best books I have ever read on publishing. I recommend reading this book even if you are not going to publish a book. The section on entrepreneurship is worth the time.

Books By Thomas Roth Jr.

Available at Amazon

The Dark Side of Photography

Floral Treasures II

Coming Soon

Floral Treasures III- available November 2013

Exit 65 - available Spring 2014

Rick's Rules- available winter 2013

Sources Quoted.

Clarie Cain Miller, NY Times. 12/08/2008 The NY Times 06/30/2013

http://www.nytimes.com/2008/12/23/business/23craft.html?pagewanted=all&_r=0

Dictionary.com 06/30/2013

http://dictionary.reference.com/browse/memorabilia

Memorabilia Madness

Memorabilia Madness